Saving Grace Money Method Mindset

Set Your Financial Life Up For Success Journal

By Grace Del Rey

Introduction

What is mindset? In the research of Carol S. Dweck, she identifies two mindsets. One is a fixed mindset and the other is a growth mindset. In a fixed mindset, the person believes that their talents and abilities are fixed. That they are as good as they are going to get. This person will want to keep the status quo at all costs whether it's to their advantage or detriment.

On the other hand, a person with a growth mindset understands and believes their talent and abilities can be developed. They don't rely on their talents alone, they believe they can change their circumstance through learning, practicing, and evaluating their failures, as well as their wins, to fully understand how to set themselves up to be the best in their endeavors.

Really, mindset is belief. You can change your mindset or belief. You can create the life of your dreams by changing your mindset.

There's a Cherokee Proverb about two wolves. There is a battle of two wolves inside us all. One is evil. It is anger, jealousy, greed, resentment, lies, inferiority, and ego. The other is good. It is joy, peace, love, hope, humanity, kindness, empathy, and truth. Which wolf will win? The one you feed.

"We are what we repeatedly do. Excellence then is not an act, but a habit."

~Aristotle~

What is your current belief about money?

"Winning at money is 80 percent behavior and 20 percent head knowledge. What to do isn't the problem; doing it is. Most of us know what to do, but we just don't do it. If I can control the guy in the mirror, I can be skinny and rich." ~ Dave Ramsey ~

Set a timer for 20 minutes and write down all your beliefs and experiences about money. Don't judge what you write, just write to hear your true belief about money. The good, the bad, and the ugly.

_____

_____

_____

_____

_____

_____

_____

_____

_____

_____

_____

_____

_____

_____

_____

_____

_____

_____

_____

_____

_____

_____

_____

What surprised you
about your beliefs
about money?

"Reflection is one of the most underused yet powerful tools for success." ~ *Richard Carlson* ~

Review what you wrote. What surprised you? Were there positive beliefs about money? Were there negative beliefs about money? Were these beliefs that you believed, because that's what your parents believed, or your friends? Are there examples of those beliefs occurring in your life, and have you had experiences where the opposite might of happened?

_____

_____

_____

_____

_____

_____

_____

_____

_____

_____

_____

_____

_____

_____

_____

_____

_____

_____

_____

_____

_____

_____

_____

_____

Explore past beliefs to give power to
what you choose
to believe going forward.

_____   _____

"It's on the strength of observation and reflection that one finds a way. So we must dig and delve unceasingly." ~ Claude Monet ~

For each of the past beliefs that do not serve you in receiving the abundance you would like to experience now, let's go through a series of prompts.

Choose one of the beliefs.

For example, "Money doesn't grow on trees." When my parents said this phrase to me, I could have interpreted it to mean a number of things:

1. I am not good enough to deserve what I was asking for.
2. What I wanted was frivolous.
3. I was being selfish.
4. There's not enough money to pay for everything.

Another example is, "You have to work hard to make money." My father believed whole heartily you had to work hard to earn money. He was a physical laborer who welded on big skyscrapers and in nuclear power plants and when he couldn't weld anymore, he drove tractor-trailer trucks. He died of a myriad of illnesses from the labor work he exposed himself to - including radiation - in an effort to provide for his family. My father had an undiagnosed learning disability known today as dyslexia. He just thought he was dumb because he could not read and write like everyone else. My father worked hard to provide for his family the best he could and he often was miserable from being tired, injured, and believing he had to sacrifice himself to make money.

Other examples of money beliefs:
1. I will lose the money.
2. I mismanage the money.
3. Someone will steal the money from me.
4. I don't deserve money, so I give it away.
5. If you have money, you must be a jerk.
6. If you have money, people will try to take advantage of you

What is one of your core beliefs about money?

_____

_____

_____

_____

_____

_____

_____

_____

How has the core belief led you to make important decisions in your life for good
or bad?

_____

_____

_____

_____

_____

_____

_____

_____

_____

If you could change this belief, what would the new belief be?

_____

_____

_____

_____

_____

_____

_____

_____

If you were to incorporate this new belief, how would your life be different?

_____
_____
_____
_____
_____
_____
_____
_____
_____
_____
_____
_____
_____
_____
_____
_____
_____
_____

What are three actions you could take this week that would support your new belief?

_____
_____
_____
_____
_____
_____
_____
_____
_____
_____
_____
_____
_____
_____
_____
_____

If you could forgive yourself for the past belief, what could you say to yourself?

_____

_____

_____

_____

_____

_____

_____

_____

_____

_____

_____

_____

If you fell back into acting from this past belief, how could you gently remind yourself of this new belief and take action to reinforce the new belief?

_____

_____

_____

_____

_____

_____

_____

_____

_____

_____

_____

_____

Please repeat this exercise as many times as you need to. The goal is to create clarity for yourself about what are the unconscious beliefs you are running on that you did not actively choose to believe but were indoctrinated into from your environment growing up. What is another of your core beliefs about money?

_____
_____
_____
_____
_____
_____
_____
_____
_____
_____

How has the core belief led you to make important decisions in your life for good or bad?

_____
_____
_____
_____
_____
_____
_____
_____

If you could change this belief, what would the new belief be?

_____
_____
_____
_____
_____
_____
_____
_____

If you were to incorporate this new belief, how would your life be different?

_____

_____

_____

_____

_____

_____

_____

_____

_____

_____

_____

_____

_____

_____

_____

_____

What are three actions you could take this week that would support your new belief?

_____

_____

_____

_____

_____

_____

_____

_____

_____

_____

_____

_____

If you could forgive yourself for the past belief, what could you say to yourself?

_____

_____

_____

_____

_____

_____

_____

_____

_____

_____

_____

_____

_____

_____

If you fell back into acting from this past belief, how could you gently remind yourself of this new belief and take action to reinforce the new belief?

_____

_____

_____

_____

_____

_____

_____

_____

_____

_____

_____

_____

By consciously monitoring your self-talk, you can change the direction of your life.

Notes:

_____

_____

_____

_____

_____

_____

_____

_____

_____

_____

_____

_____

_____

_____

_____

_____

_____

_____

_____

_____

_____

_____

_____

_____

_____

_____

_____

_____

What is your
WHY?

"He who has a why to live, can bear almost any how." ~ Friedrich Nietzsche ~

What is your why?

Why do what you do? Why do you want money? What would you do with the money you received? What experience would you want to create with the money you received? Who would you help if allowed?

Set a timer for 30 minutes and really explore if you had all the money in the world, what would you do with it and what would be at the core of your WHY?

_____

_____

_____

_____

_____

_____

_____

_____

_____

_____

_____

_____

_____

_____

_____

_____

_____

_____

_____

_____

_____

_____

_____

Vision Board

"Nothing is impossible, the word itself says 'I'm possible'!" ~ Audrey Hepburn ~

In my life, I have made a dozen vision boards. I first made a vision board when working through The Artist Way by Julian Cameron.

Ps. I highly recommend her book as an exploration to uncovering your inner artist.

Set a timer and write about the life you would live if money was not an issue. What would your life look like? Then take the time to print or clip images from magazines and paste the images onto a poster board or canvas. Don't limit yourself. Just have fun knowing anything is possible if you allow it. Hang your vision board where you can see it daily.

_____

_____

_____

_____

_____

_____

_____

_____

_____

_____

_____

_____

_____

_____

_____

_____

_____

_____

_____

_____

_____

_____

_____

Positive Affirmations & Law
of Attractions

"Just one small positive thought in the morning can change your whole day." ~ Dalai Lama ~

One of the most powerful tools I use on a daily basis is positive affirmations. I learned it from Chellie Campbell and her book "The Wealthy Spirit". There was a time in my life when I was so short on cash, I didn't have rent, money for groceries, or utilities, and not sure where that money was going to come from.

I met Chellie Campbell at a networking event and was drawn to what she was selling in terms of growing and running a business. I didn't have money for her class and I remember crying on the phone to her about how broke I was. She held her boundary on the price for her course, but she told me to get her book "The Wealthy Spirit" and start incorporating the affirmation in my life. I did and a month later was enrolled in her course which propelled me forward in my budding accounting business.

There's a trick to the positive affirmation, you have to genuinely believe in what you are repeating or you will not be able to attract or be the thing you are saying. Abraham-Hicks has wonderful teachings on the Law of Attraction with books and speaking events. There was a story Esther Hicks was recounting about air travel. She was stuck on a plane because the passenger boarding bridge had a gap between it and the doorway. She was experiencing anxiety about missing her connecting flight home. She used the analogy of the gap to get off the plane and the passenger boarding bridge to that of one's mind being in a negative space like "I never have enough money to pay off my credit card debts."

To have a positive mindset, "I always have more than enough money." Esther sited to build your own bridge over the gap, one had to look at examples in their lives where they did have enough money, and in her case, she started to recall all the times she had traveled and always made her connecting flights with no delays. As she recounted all the positive flight experiences she had, her anxiety went down, and the passenger boarding bridge finally closed the gap, so she and Jerry could deplane to catch their connecting flight.

I discovered that in my own life, a few things hold true. One, the inner voice you hear in your head will tell you lies and judge you harsher than anyone outside of you. The inner voice is often your ego trying to keep you safe from the perceived harm you might face if you change, succeed and obtain the wealth you are wanting to experience in the now.

You can only have one thought active in your mind at a time. You can either let your ego voice run amuck in your head, or you can choose what your mind is thinking and programming to attract in your life. When I found I was worrying about money almost obsessively and hyperfocused on not enough, I would catch myself and start to repeat in mantra-like style my go-to affirmations that I believed - because I had experienced them at least once.

For example, I often use "I am a money magnet." Because I have often attracted money by enrolling new clients, finishing a project, and receiving gifts in the mail via residual from past acting work. I don't focus on the "how" to get the money but on the experience of what it feels like to obtain the dream.

Another affirmation I like to use is, "My clients praise me and pay me." This one came to me at a time when I had loads of clients but was having a difficult time receiving payment. So to contour balance what I was experiencing, I would start to chant this affirmation and within a short period of time, the checks would show up in my mailbox.

So I invite you to come up with a list of affirmations that can be your go-to mantras when you find yourself having negative self-talk, in a downward spiral of your current circumstance, or struggling with a particular goal. The affirmation doesn't replace you taking inspired action toward your goal every day, but the affirmation assists with clearing the path for you to receive what you are endeavoring to obtain.

When creating your own affirmations, write your affirmation in a positive creation. For example, if I wrote, " I don't want any debt," or "I don't want to feel tired." The law attraction only sees "Oh you want more debt and to be tired, okay here you go, I will send more of those experiences to you." To flip it to a positive creation, I would write, "I am filled with vital energy." And "I still have plenty of money after my bills are all paid."

Here are a few affirmations to get you started:

1. I am filled with vital energy and easily accomplish my goals.
2. My clients praise me and pay me.
3. I still have plenty of money after my bills are paid.
4. I now earn a great big income doing what makes me happy.
5. Money flows easily and effortlessly to me.
6. I am endlessly creative and money flows effortlessly to me.
7. The more fun I have the more money I make!
8. The more I give, the more I receive, for both are infinite.
9. I have all the time I need to have all the fun I want.
10. I am a money magnet.
11. I am grateful for all the abundance in my life.

_____

_____

_____

_____

_____

_____

_____

_____

_____

_____

_____

_____

_____

_____

_____

_____

_____

_____

_____

_____

_____

Daily Practice

"You'll never change your life until you change something you do daily. The secret to your success is found in your daily routine." ~ John C. Maxwell ~

Practice makes perfect, so spend the next 30 days putting into practice envisioning experiences you have created on your vision board. Write down inspired actions that move you toward accomplishing your goal. Seek out how many different ways you can practice your top 5 affirmations daily. Journal about your experiences as a reflection of what you are attracting into your life.

Write below what your daily practice would look like and how much time you would need if you only had 5 minutes, and then if you only had 10 minutes, and then if you had 20 minutes. Work your way up to 30 minutes to an hour. I highly recommend creating your day each day with your set intentions. Because life gets busy, set yourself up for success by knowing what you could do in your daily practice if you only had 5 or 10 minutes.

_____

_____

_____

_____

_____

_____

_____

_____

_____

_____

_____

_____

_____

_____

_____

_____

_____

Daily Plan

DATE

S M T W T F S

Today's Goals

Energy Level

Priorities

Wins

Moments of Gratitude

MANIFESTATION TECHNIQUE USED

TRIGGERING EVENT: _____

SUCCESS TRACKER

NEGATIVE LIMITING BELIEFS: _____

○ _____

○ _____

○ _____

Cardio workout	○	○	○	○	○	○
Meditation	○	○	○	○	○	○
Yoga	○	○	○	○	○	○
Went for a walk	○	○	○	○	○	○
Met a friend	○	○	○	○	○	○
Social Media break	○	○	○	○	○	○
Medication	○	○	○	○	○	○
Cardio workout	○	○	○	○	○	○
Meditation	○	○	○	○	○	○
Yoga	○	○	○	○	○	○
Went for a walk	○	○	○	○	○	○
Met a friend	○	○	○	○	○	○
Social Media break	○	○	○	○	○	○
Medication	○	○	○	○	○	○

POSITIVE AFFIRMATIONS _____

○ _____

○ _____

○ _____

NOTES

Daily Plan

DATE

S M T W T F S

Today's Goals

Energy Level

Priorities

Wins

Moments of Gratitude

MANIFESTATION TECHNIQUE USED

TRIGGERING EVENT: _____

SUCCESS TRACKER

NEGATIVE LIMITING BELIEFS: _____

○ _____

○ _____

○ _____

Cardio workout	○	○	○	○	○	○
Meditation	○	○	○	○	○	○
Yoga	○	○	○	○	○	○
Went for a walk	○	○	○	○	○	○
Met a friend	○	○	○	○	○	○
Social Media break	○	○	○	○	○	○
Medication	○	○	○	○	○	○
Cardio workout	○	○	○	○	○	○
Meditation	○	○	○	○	○	○
Yoga	○	○	○	○	○	○
Went for a walk	○	○	○	○	○	○
Met a friend	○	○	○	○	○	○
Social Media break	○	○	○	○	○	○
Medication	○	○	○	○	○	○

POSITIVE AFFIRMATIONS _____

○ _____

○ _____

○ _____

NOTES

Daily Plan

DATE   S M T W T F S

Today's Goals

Energy Level

Priorities

Wins

Moments of Gratitude

MANIFESTATION TECHNIQUE USED

TRIGGERING EVENT: _____

SUCCESS TRACKER

NEGATIVE LIMITING BELIEFS: _____

○ _____

_____

○ _____

_____

○ _____

_____

Cardio workout	○	○	○	○	○	○
Meditation	○	○	○	○	○	○
Yoga	○	○	○	○	○	○
Went for a walk	○	○	○	○	○	○
Met a friend	○	○	○	○	○	○
Social Media break	○	○	○	○	○	○
Medication	○	○	○	○	○	○
Cardio workout	○	○	○	○	○	○
Meditation	○	○	○	○	○	○
Yoga	○	○	○	○	○	○
Went for a walk	○	○	○	○	○	○
Met a friend	○	○	○	○	○	○
Social Media break	○	○	○	○	○	○
Medication	○	○	○	○	○	○

POSITIVE AFFIRMATIONS _____

○ _____

_____

○ _____

_____

○ _____

_____

NOTES

Daily Plan

DATE   S M T W T F S

Today's Goals

Energy Level

Priorities

Wins

Moments of Gratitude

MANIFESTATION TECHNIQUE USED

TRIGGERING EVENT: _____

SUCCESS TRACKER

NEGATIVE LIMITING BELIEFS: _____

○ _____

○ _____

○ _____

Cardio workout	○	○	○	○	○	○
Meditation	○	○	○	○	○	○
Yoga	○	○	○	○	○	○
Went for a walk	○	○	○	○	○	○
Met a friend	○	○	○	○	○	○
Social Media break	○	○	○	○	○	○
Medication	○	○	○	○	○	○
Cardio workout	○	○	○	○	○	○
Meditation	○	○	○	○	○	○
Yoga	○	○	○	○	○	○
Went for a walk	○	○	○	○	○	○
Met a friend	○	○	○	○	○	○
Social Media break	○	○	○	○	○	○
Medication	○	○	○	○	○	○

POSITIVE AFFIRMATIONS _____

○ _____

○ _____

○ _____

NOTES

Daily Plan

DATE   S M T W T F S

Today's Goals

Energy Level

Priorities

Wins

Moments of Gratitude

MANIFESTATION TECHNIQUE USED

TRIGGERING EVENT:

SUCCESS TRACKER

NEGATIVE LIMITING BELIEFS:

○ _____
○ _____
○ _____

Cardio workout	○	○	○	○	○	○
Meditation	○	○	○	○	○	○
Yoga	○	○	○	○	○	○
Went for a walk	○	○	○	○	○	○
Met a friend	○	○	○	○	○	○
Social Media break	○	○	○	○	○	○
Medication	○	○	○	○	○	○
Cardio workout	○	○	○	○	○	○
Meditation	○	○	○	○	○	○
Yoga	○	○	○	○	○	○
Went for a walk	○	○	○	○	○	○
Met a friend	○	○	○	○	○	○
Social Media break	○	○	○	○	○	○
Medication	○	○	○	○	○	○

POSITIVE AFFIRMATIONS

○ _____
○ _____
○ _____

NOTES

Daily Plan

DATE   S M T W T F S

Today's Goals

Energy Level

Priorities

Wins

Moments of Gratitude

MANIFESTATION TECHNIQUE USED

TRIGGERING EVENT: _____

SUCCESS TRACKER

NEGATIVE LIMITING BELIEFS: _____

○ _____

○ _____

○ _____

Cardio workout	○	○	○	○	○	○
Meditation	○	○	○	○	○	○
Yoga	○	○	○	○	○	○
Went for a walk	○	○	○	○	○	○
Met a friend	○	○	○	○	○	○
Social Media break	○	○	○	○	○	○
Medication	○	○	○	○	○	○
Cardio workout	○	○	○	○	○	○
Meditation	○	○	○	○	○	○
Yoga	○	○	○	○	○	○
Went for a walk	○	○	○	○	○	○
Met a friend	○	○	○	○	○	○
Social Media break	○	○	○	○	○	○
Medication	○	○	○	○	○	○

POSITIVE AFFIRMATIONS _____

○ _____

○ _____

○ _____

NOTES

Daily Plan

DATE   S M T W T F S

Today's Goals

Energy Level

Priorities

Wins

Moments of Gratitude

MANIFESTATION TECHNIQUE USED _____   TRIGGERING EVENT: _____

SUCCESS TRACKER

NEGATIVE LIMITING BELIEFS: _____

○ _____

○ _____

○ _____

Cardio workout	○	○	○	○	○	○
Meditation	○	○	○	○	○	○
Yoga	○	○	○	○	○	○
Went for a walk	○	○	○	○	○	○
Met a friend	○	○	○	○	○	○
Social Media break	○	○	○	○	○	○
Medication	○	○	○	○	○	○
Cardio workout	○	○	○	○	○	○
Meditation	○	○	○	○	○	○
Yoga	○	○	○	○	○	○
Went for a walk	○	○	○	○	○	○
Met a friend	○	○	○	○	○	○
Social Media break	○	○	○	○	○	○
Medication	○	○	○	○	○	○

POSITIVE AFFIRMATIONS _____

○ _____

○ _____

○ _____

NOTES

[ ]

Daily Plan

DATE _____   S M T W T F S

Today's Goals

Energy Level

Priorities

Wins

Moments of Gratitude

MANIFESTATION TECHNIQUE USED _____

TRIGGERING EVENT: _____

NEGATIVE LIMITING BELIEFS: _____

○ _____

○ _____

○ _____

POSITIVE AFFIRMATIONS _____

○ _____

○ _____

○ _____

SUCCESS TRACKER

Cardio workout	○	○	○	○	○	○
Meditation	○	○	○	○	○	○
Yoga	○	○	○	○	○	○
Went for a walk	○	○	○	○	○	○
Met a friend	○	○	○	○	○	○
Social Media break	○	○	○	○	○	○
Medication	○	○	○	○	○	○
Cardio workout	○	○	○	○	○	○
Meditation	○	○	○	○	○	○
Yoga	○	○	○	○	○	○
Went for a walk	○	○	○	○	○	○
Met a friend	○	○	○	○	○	○
Social Media break	○	○	○	○	○	○
Medication	○	○	○	○	○	○

NOTES

Daily Plan

DATE   S M T W T F S

Today's Goals

Energy Level

Priorities

Wins

Moments of Gratitude

MANIFESTATION TECHNIQUE USED

TRIGGERING EVENT: _____

SUCCESS TRACKER

NEGATIVE LIMITING BELIEFS: _____

○ _____

○ _____

○ _____

POSITIVE AFFIRMATIONS _____

○ _____

○ _____

○ _____

Cardio workout	○	○	○	○	○	○
Meditation	○	○	○	○	○	○
Yoga	○	○	○	○	○	○
Went for a walk	○	○	○	○	○	○
Met a friend	○	○	○	○	○	○
Social Media break	○	○	○	○	○	○
Medication	○	○	○	○	○	○
Cardio workout	○	○	○	○	○	○
Meditation	○	○	○	○	○	○
Yoga	○	○	○	○	○	○
Went for a walk	○	○	○	○	○	○
Met a friend	○	○	○	○	○	○
Social Media break	○	○	○	○	○	○
Medication	○	○	○	○	○	○

NOTES

Daily Plan

DATE   S M T W T F S

Today's Goals

Energy Level

Priorities

Wins

Moments of Gratitude

MANIFESTATION TECHNIQUE USED

TRIGGERING EVENT: _____

SUCCESS TRACKER

NEGATIVE LIMITING BELIEFS: _____

○ _____

○ _____

○ _____

Cardio workout	○	○	○	○	○	○
Meditation	○	○	○	○	○	○
Yoga	○	○	○	○	○	○
Went for a walk	○	○	○	○	○	○
Met a friend	○	○	○	○	○	○
Social Media break	○	○	○	○	○	○
Medication	○	○	○	○	○	○
Cardio workout	○	○	○	○	○	○
Meditation	○	○	○	○	○	○
Yoga	○	○	○	○	○	○
Went for a walk	○	○	○	○	○	○
Met a friend	○	○	○	○	○	○
Social Media break	○	○	○	○	○	○
Medication	○	○	○	○	○	○

POSITIVE AFFIRMATIONS _____

○ _____

○ _____

○ _____

NOTES

Daily Plan

DATE   S M T W T F S

Today's Goals

Energy Level

Priorities

Wins

Moments of Gratitude

MANIFESTATION TECHNIQUE USED

TRIGGERING EVENT: _____

SUCCESS TRACKER

NEGATIVE LIMITING BELIEFS: _____

○ _____

○ _____

○ _____

Cardio workout	○	○	○	○	○	○
Meditation	○	○	○	○	○	○
Yoga	○	○	○	○	○	○
Went for a walk	○	○	○	○	○	○
Met a friend	○	○	○	○	○	○
Social Media break	○	○	○	○	○	○
Medication	○	○	○	○	○	○
Cardio workout	○	○	○	○	○	○
Meditation	○	○	○	○	○	○
Yoga	○	○	○	○	○	○
Went for a walk	○	○	○	○	○	○
Met a friend	○	○	○	○	○	○
Social Media break	○	○	○	○	○	○
Medication	○	○	○	○	○	○

POSITIVE AFFIRMATIONS _____

○ _____

○ _____

○ _____

NOTES

Daily Plan

DATE   S M T W T F S

Today's Goals

Energy Level

Priorities

Wins

Moments of Gratitude

MANIFESTATION TECHNIQUE USED

TRIGGERING EVENT: _____

SUCCESS TRACKER

NEGATIVE LIMITING BELIEFS: _____

- ○ _____
- ○ _____
- ○ _____

POSITIVE AFFIRMATIONS _____

- ○ _____
- ○ _____
- ○ _____

Cardio workout	○	○	○	○	○	○
Meditation	○	○	○	○	○	○
Yoga	○	○	○	○	○	○
Went for a walk	○	○	○	○	○	○
Met a friend	○	○	○	○	○	○
Social Media break	○	○	○	○	○	○
Medication	○	○	○	○	○	○
Cardio workout	○	○	○	○	○	○
Meditation	○	○	○	○	○	○
Yoga	○	○	○	○	○	○
Went for a walk	○	○	○	○	○	○
Met a friend	○	○	○	○	○	○
Social Media break	○	○	○	○	○	○
Medication	○	○	○	○	○	○

NOTES

Daily Plan

DATE   S M T W T F S

Today's Goals

Energy Level

Priorities

Wins

Moments of Gratitude

MANIFESTATION TECHNIQUE USED

TRIGGERING EVENT: _____

NEGATIVE LIMITING BELIEFS:

○ _____

○ _____

○ _____

POSITIVE AFFIRMATIONS

○ _____

○ _____

○ _____

SUCCESS TRACKER

Cardio workout	○	○	○	○	○	○
Meditation	○	○	○	○	○	○
Yoga	○	○	○	○	○	○
Went for a walk	○	○	○	○	○	○
Met a friend	○	○	○	○	○	○
Social Media break	○	○	○	○	○	○
Medication	○	○	○	○	○	○
Cardio workout	○	○	○	○	○	○
Meditation	○	○	○	○	○	○
Yoga	○	○	○	○	○	○
Went for a walk	○	○	○	○	○	○
Met a friend	○	○	○	○	○	○
Social Media break	○	○	○	○	○	○
Medication	○	○	○	○	○	○

NOTES

Daily Plan

DATE

S M T W T F S

Today's Goals

Energy Level

Priorities

Wins

Moments of Gratitude

MANIFESTATION TECHNIQUE USED _____   TRIGGERING EVENT: _____

SUCCESS TRACKER

NEGATIVE LIMITING BELIEFS: _____

○ _____

○ _____

○ _____

POSITIVE AFFIRMATIONS _____

○ _____

○ _____

○ _____

Cardio workout	○	○	○	○	○	○
Meditation	○	○	○	○	○	○
Yoga	○	○	○	○	○	○
Went for a walk	○	○	○	○	○	○
Met a friend	○	○	○	○	○	○
Social Media break	○	○	○	○	○	○
Medication	○	○	○	○	○	○
Cardio workout	○	○	○	○	○	○
Meditation	○	○	○	○	○	○
Yoga	○	○	○	○	○	○
Went for a walk	○	○	○	○	○	○
Met a friend	○	○	○	○	○	○
Social Media break	○	○	○	○	○	○
Medication	○	○	○	○	○	○

NOTES

Daily Plan

DATE   S M T W T F S

Today's Goals

Energy Level

Priorities

Wins

Moments of Gratitude

MANIFESTATION TECHNIQUE USED

TRIGGERING EVENT: _____

SUCCESS TRACKER

NEGATIVE LIMITING BELIEFS: _____

- ○ _____
- ○ _____
- ○ _____

POSITIVE AFFIRMATIONS _____

- ○ _____
- ○ _____
- ○ _____

Cardio workout	○	○	○	○	○	○
Meditation	○	○	○	○	○	○
Yoga	○	○	○	○	○	○
Went for a walk	○	○	○	○	○	○
Met a friend	○	○	○	○	○	○
Social Media break	○	○	○	○	○	○
Medication	○	○	○	○	○	○
Cardio workout	○	○	○	○	○	○
Meditation	○	○	○	○	○	○
Yoga	○	○	○	○	○	○
Went for a walk	○	○	○	○	○	○
Met a friend	○	○	○	○	○	○
Social Media break	○	○	○	○	○	○
Medication	○	○	○	○	○	○

NOTES

Daily Plan

DATE   S M T W T F S

Today's Goals

Energy Level

Priorities

Wins

Moments of Gratitude

MANIFESTATION TECHNIQUE USED

TRIGGERING EVENT:

SUCCESS TRACKER

NEGATIVE LIMITING BELIEFS:

○ _____

○ _____

○ _____

POSITIVE AFFIRMATIONS

○ _____

○ _____

○ _____

Cardio workout	○	○	○	○	○	○
Meditation	○	○	○	○	○	○
Yoga	○	○	○	○	○	○
Went for a walk	○	○	○	○	○	○
Met a friend	○	○	○	○	○	○
Social Media break	○	○	○	○	○	○
Medication	○	○	○	○	○	○
Cardio workout	○	○	○	○	○	○
Meditation	○	○	○	○	○	○
Yoga	○	○	○	○	○	○
Went for a walk	○	○	○	○	○	○
Met a friend	○	○	○	○	○	○
Social Media break	○	○	○	○	○	○
Medication	○	○	○	○	○	○

NOTES

Daily Plan

DATE   S M T W T F S

Today's Goals

Energy Level

Priorities

Wins

Moments of Gratitude

MANIFESTATION TECHNIQUE USED _____   TRIGGERING EVENT: _____

SUCCESS TRACKER

NEGATIVE LIMITING BELIEFS: _____

○ _____

○ _____

○ _____

Cardio workout	○	○	○	○	○	○
Meditation	○	○	○	○	○	○
Yoga	○	○	○	○	○	○
Went for a walk	○	○	○	○	○	○
Met a friend	○	○	○	○	○	○
Social Media break	○	○	○	○	○	○
Medication	○	○	○	○	○	○
Cardio workout	○	○	○	○	○	○
Meditation	○	○	○	○	○	○
Yoga	○	○	○	○	○	○
Went for a walk	○	○	○	○	○	○
Met a friend	○	○	○	○	○	○
Social Media break	○	○	○	○	○	○
Medication	○	○	○	○	○	○

POSITIVE AFFIRMATIONS _____

○ _____

○ _____

○ _____

NOTES

Daily Plan

DATE   S M T W T F S

Today's Goals

Energy Level

Priorities

Wins

Moments of Gratitude

MANIFESTATION TECHNIQUE USED _____

TRIGGERING EVENT: _____

NEGATIVE LIMITING BELIEFS: _____

- ○ _____
- ○ _____
- ○ _____

POSITIVE AFFIRMATIONS _____

- ○ _____
- ○ _____
- ○ _____

SUCCESS TRACKER

Cardio workout	○	○	○	○	○	○
Meditation	○	○	○	○	○	○
Yoga	○	○	○	○	○	○
Went for a walk	○	○	○	○	○	○
Met a friend	○	○	○	○	○	○
Social Media break	○	○	○	○	○	○
Medication	○	○	○	○	○	○
Cardio workout	○	○	○	○	○	○
Meditation	○	○	○	○	○	○
Yoga	○	○	○	○	○	○
Went for a walk	○	○	○	○	○	○
Met a friend	○	○	○	○	○	○
Social Media break	○	○	○	○	○	○
Medication	○	○	○	○	○	○

NOTES

Daily Plan

DATE   S M T W T F S

Today's Goals

Energy Level

Priorities

Wins

Moments of Gratitude

MANIFESTATION TECHNIQUE USED

TRIGGERING EVENT: _____

NEGATIVE LIMITING BELIEFS: _____

- ○ _____
- ○ _____
- ○ _____

POSITIVE AFFIRMATIONS _____

- ○ _____
- ○ _____
- ○ _____

SUCCESS TRACKER

Cardio workout	○	○	○	○	○	○	○
Meditation	○	○	○	○	○	○	○
Yoga	○	○	○	○	○	○	○
Went for a walk	○	○	○	○	○	○	○
Met a friend	○	○	○	○	○	○	○
Social Media break	○	○	○	○	○	○	○
Medication	○	○	○	○	○	○	○
Cardio workout	○	○	○	○	○	○	○
Meditation	○	○	○	○	○	○	○
Yoga	○	○	○	○	○	○	○
Went for a walk	○	○	○	○	○	○	○
Met a friend	○	○	○	○	○	○	○
Social Media break	○	○	○	○	○	○	○
Medication	○	○	○	○	○	○	○

NOTES

Daily Plan

DATE

S M T W T F S

Today's Goals

Energy Level

Priorities

Wins

Moments of Gratitude

MANIFESTATION TECHNIQUE USED _____

TRIGGERING EVENT: _____

SUCCESS TRACKER

NEGATIVE LIMITING BELIEFS: _____

○ _____

○ _____

○ _____

Cardio workout	○	○	○	○	○	○
Meditation	○	○	○	○	○	○
Yoga	○	○	○	○	○	○
Went for a walk	○	○	○	○	○	○
Met a friend	○	○	○	○	○	○
Social Media break	○	○	○	○	○	○
Medication	○	○	○	○	○	○
Cardio workout	○	○	○	○	○	○
Meditation	○	○	○	○	○	○
Yoga	○	○	○	○	○	○
Went for a walk	○	○	○	○	○	○
Met a friend	○	○	○	○	○	○
Social Media break	○	○	○	○	○	○
Medication	○	○	○	○	○	○

POSITIVE AFFIRMATIONS _____

○ _____

○ _____

○ _____

NOTES

Daily Plan

S M T W T F S

Today's Goals

Energy Level

Priorities

Wins

Moments of Gratitude

MANIFESTATION TECHNIQUE USED

TRIGGERING EVENT: _____

SUCCESS TRACKER

NEGATIVE LIMITING BELIEFS: _____

○ _____

○ _____

○ _____

POSITIVE AFFIRMATIONS _____

○ _____

○ _____

○ _____

Cardio workout	○	○	○	○	○	○
Meditation	○	○	○	○	○	○
Yoga	○	○	○	○	○	○
Went for a walk	○	○	○	○	○	○
Met a friend	○	○	○	○	○	○
Social Media break	○	○	○	○	○	○
Medication	○	○	○	○	○	○
Cardio workout	○	○	○	○	○	○
Meditation	○	○	○	○	○	○
Yoga	○	○	○	○	○	○
Went for a walk	○	○	○	○	○	○
Met a friend	○	○	○	○	○	○
Social Media break	○	○	○	○	○	○
Medication	○	○	○	○	○	○

NOTES

Daily Plan

DATE   S M T W T F S

Today's Goals

Energy Level

Priorities

Wins

Moments of Gratitude

MANIFESTATION TECHNIQUE USED

TRIGGERING EVENT: _____

NEGATIVE LIMITING BELIEFS: _____

○ _____

○ _____

○ _____

POSITIVE AFFIRMATIONS _____

○ _____

○ _____

○ _____

SUCCESS TRACKER

Cardio workout	○	○	○	○	○	○	○
Meditation	○	○	○	○	○	○	○
Yoga	○	○	○	○	○	○	○
Went for a walk	○	○	○	○	○	○	○
Met a friend	○	○	○	○	○	○	○
Social Media break	○	○	○	○	○	○	○
Medication	○	○	○	○	○	○	○
Cardio workout	○	○	○	○	○	○	○
Meditation	○	○	○	○	○	○	○
Yoga	○	○	○	○	○	○	○
Went for a walk	○	○	○	○	○	○	○
Met a friend	○	○	○	○	○	○	○
Social Media break	○	○	○	○	○	○	○
Medication	○	○	○	○	○	○	○

NOTES

Daily Plan

DATE   S M T W T F S

Today's Goals

Energy Level

Priorities

Wins

Moments of Gratitude

MANIFESTATION TECHNIQUE USED

TRIGGERING EVENT: _____

SUCCESS TRACKER

NEGATIVE LIMITING BELIEFS: _____

○ _____

○ _____

○ _____

Cardio workout	○	○	○	○	○	○
Meditation	○	○	○	○	○	○
Yoga	○	○	○	○	○	○
Went for a walk	○	○	○	○	○	○
Met a friend	○	○	○	○	○	○
Social Media break	○	○	○	○	○	○
Medication	○	○	○	○	○	○
Cardio workout	○	○	○	○	○	○
Meditation	○	○	○	○	○	○
Yoga	○	○	○	○	○	○
Went for a walk	○	○	○	○	○	○
Met a friend	○	○	○	○	○	○
Social Media break	○	○	○	○	○	○
Medication	○	○	○	○	○	○

POSITIVE AFFIRMATIONS _____

○ _____

○ _____

○ _____

NOTES

Daily Plan

DATE   S M T W T F S

Today's Goals

Energy Level

Priorities

Wins

Moments of Gratitude

MANIFESTATION TECHNIQUE USED

TRIGGERING EVENT: _____

SUCCESS TRACKER

NEGATIVE LIMITING BELIEFS: _____

○ _____

○ _____

○ _____

POSITIVE AFFIRMATIONS _____

○ _____

○ _____

○ _____

Cardio workout   ○ ○ ○ ○ ○ ○ ○

Meditation   ○ ○ ○ ○ ○ ○ ○

Yoga   ○ ○ ○ ○ ○ ○ ○

Went for a walk   ○ ○ ○ ○ ○ ○ ○

Met a friend   ○ ○ ○ ○ ○ ○ ○

Social Media break   ○ ○ ○ ○ ○ ○ ○

Medication   ○ ○ ○ ○ ○ ○ ○

Cardio workout   ○ ○ ○ ○ ○ ○ ○

Meditation   ○ ○ ○ ○ ○ ○ ○

Yoga   ○ ○ ○ ○ ○ ○ ○

Went for a walk   ○ ○ ○ ○ ○ ○ ○

Met a friend   ○ ○ ○ ○ ○ ○ ○

Social Media break   ○ ○ ○ ○ ○ ○ ○

Medication   ○ ○ ○ ○ ○ ○ ○

NOTES

Daily Plan

Today's Goals

Energy Level

Priorities

Wins

Moments of Gratitude

MANIFESTATION TECHNIQUE USED _____

TRIGGERING EVENT: _____

SUCCESS TRACKER

NEGATIVE LIMITING BELIEFS: _____

○ _____

○ _____

○ _____

POSITIVE AFFIRMATIONS _____

○ _____

○ _____

○ _____

Cardio workout	○	○	○	○	○	○
Meditation	○	○	○	○	○	○
Yoga	○	○	○	○	○	○
Went for a walk	○	○	○	○	○	○
Met a friend	○	○	○	○	○	○
Social Media break	○	○	○	○	○	○
Medication	○	○	○	○	○	○
Cardio workout	○	○	○	○	○	○
Meditation	○	○	○	○	○	○
Yoga	○	○	○	○	○	○
Went for a walk	○	○	○	○	○	○
Met a friend	○	○	○	○	○	○
Social Media break	○	○	○	○	○	○
Medication	○	○	○	○	○	○

NOTES

Daily Plan

DATE   S M T W T F S

Today's Goals

Energy Level

Priorities

Wins

Moments of Gratitude

MANIFESTATION TECHNIQUE USED

TRIGGERING EVENT: _____

SUCCESS TRACKER

NEGATIVE LIMITING BELIEFS: _____

○ _____

○ _____

○ _____

POSITIVE AFFIRMATIONS _____

○ _____

○ _____

○ _____

Cardio workout	○	○	○	○	○	○	○
Meditation	○	○	○	○	○	○	○
Yoga	○	○	○	○	○	○	○
Went for a walk	○	○	○	○	○	○	○
Met a friend	○	○	○	○	○	○	○
Social Media break	○	○	○	○	○	○	○
Medication	○	○	○	○	○	○	○
Cardio workout	○	○	○	○	○	○	○
Meditation	○	○	○	○	○	○	○
Yoga	○	○	○	○	○	○	○
Went for a walk	○	○	○	○	○	○	○
Met a friend	○	○	○	○	○	○	○
Social Media break	○	○	○	○	○	○	○
Medication	○	○	○	○	○	○	○

NOTES

Daily Plan

DATE   S M T W T F S

Today's Goals

Energy Level

Priorities

Wins

Moments of Gratitude

MANIFESTATION TECHNIQUE USED _____   TRIGGERING EVENT: _____

SUCCESS TRACKER

NEGATIVE LIMITING BELIEFS: _____

○ _____

○ _____

○ _____

POSITIVE AFFIRMATIONS _____

○ _____

○ _____

○ _____

Cardio workout	○	○	○	○	○	○
Meditation	○	○	○	○	○	○
Yoga	○	○	○	○	○	○
Went for a walk	○	○	○	○	○	○
Met a friend	○	○	○	○	○	○
Social Media break	○	○	○	○	○	○
Medication	○	○	○	○	○	○
Cardio workout	○	○	○	○	○	○
Meditation	○	○	○	○	○	○
Yoga	○	○	○	○	○	○
Went for a walk	○	○	○	○	○	○
Met a friend	○	○	○	○	○	○
Social Media break	○	○	○	○	○	○
Medication	○	○	○	○	○	○

NOTES

Daily Plan

DATE   S   M   T   W   T   F   S

Today's Goals

Energy Level

Priorities

Wins

Moments of Gratitude

MANIFESTATION TECHNIQUE USED _____

TRIGGERING EVENT: _____

SUCCESS TRACKER

NEGATIVE LIMITING BELIEFS: _____

○ _____
_____
○ _____
_____
○ _____
_____

POSITIVE AFFIRMATIONS _____

○ _____
_____
○ _____
_____
○ _____
_____

Cardio workout	○	○	○	○	○	○ ○
Meditation	○	○	○	○	○	○ ○
Yoga	○	○	○	○	○	○ ○
Went for a walk	○	○	○	○	○	○ ○
Met a friend	○	○	○	○	○	○ ○
Social Media break	○	○	○	○	○	○ ○
Medication	○	○	○	○	○	○ ○
Cardio workout	○	○	○	○	○	○ ○
Meditation	○	○	○	○	○	○ ○
Yoga	○	○	○	○	○	○ ○
Went for a walk	○	○	○	○	○	○ ○
Met a friend	○	○	○	○	○	○ ○
Social Media break	○	○	○	○	○	○ ○
Medication	○	○	○	○	○	○ ○

NOTES

Daily Plan

DATE   S M T W T F S

Today's Goals

Energy Level

Priorities

Wins

Moments of Gratitude

MANIFESTATION TECHNIQUE USED _____   TRIGGERING EVENT: _____

SUCCESS TRACKER

NEGATIVE LIMITING BELIEFS: _____

○ _____

○ _____

○ _____

Cardio workout	○	○	○	○	○	○
Meditation	○	○	○	○	○	○
Yoga	○	○	○	○	○	○
Went for a walk	○	○	○	○	○	○
Met a friend	○	○	○	○	○	○
Social Media break	○	○	○	○	○	○
Medication	○	○	○	○	○	○
Cardio workout	○	○	○	○	○	○
Meditation	○	○	○	○	○	○
Yoga	○	○	○	○	○	○
Went for a walk	○	○	○	○	○	○
Met a friend	○	○	○	○	○	○
Social Media break	○	○	○	○	○	○
Medication	○	○	○	○	○	○

POSITIVE AFFIRMATIONS _____

○ _____

○ _____

○ _____

NOTES